LEARNING
ROOTS

HAJJ and UMRAH
Activity Book

This book belongs to

....

NOTES FOR GROWN-UPS

Who Is This Book Suitable for?

This book contains activities for 8-10 year olds.

Your Feedback is MORE Than Welcome!

Every effort has been made to ensure the information contained in this pack is accurate, authentic and pedagogically sound. If you find anything to the contrary, we welcome your feedback at: **www.learningroots.com/feedback**

Stickers, Cut-Out & Pull-Out pages

In order to make learning fun and varied, some of the activities in this book require the use of stickers, cut-out objects and pull-out pages. All of these sections are clearly labelled in the book and are referenced on the contents pages. Please ensure you supervise your child when cutting objects from the cut-out pages, or have an adult cut it for them. Similarly, please keep the stickers out of reach from small children under the age of 3 years.

Suggestions on How to Use this Book

We highly recommend that you **be present to support your child** while they do the activities, in order to foster, create and cherish quality faith-filled moments with your child.

Sharing or Copying Pages from this Book

For the best experience, this publication has been designed to be used by one child. If you would like to use this book with more than one child, such as a large household or a class of children at an educational institution, please purchase one book for every child. Please contact us at **support@learningroots.com** for details on our discounts for educational institutions. Otherwise, no part of this publication may be reproduced, stored in a retrieval system, or transmitted, in any form, or by any means, electronic, mechanical, photocopying, recording or otherwise without prior written permission from Learning Roots.

Some activities require a **grown-up** to help explain or read instructions.

Simple reference numbers for you to find your way.

Four categories cover the main topics in Hajj.

Excellent effort!

SACRED RITES

75

From All Around the World

Layla sees Muslims from all around the world in Arafah. Learn about where they are from by matching the **stickers** to the correct scenes.

OBSERVATION SKILLS

Key skills are used to develop your child holistically.

Some activities make use of **stickers** which you can find at the back of the book.

CONTENTS

Meet the Families

- These families are going on Hajj! For each family, match the character names in English with the Arabic names using the **stickers**. You'll be meeting the families again in the activities to come!

زيد

ثابت

عائشة

سارة

صفية

هبة

ليث

قيس

TRAVEL JOY

Remember Your Passport!

● Follow the steps below to make your own Hajj passport. You'll be collecting stamps in your passport showing all the wonderful places you'll visit during your journey.

1 With the help of a **grown-up**, use scissors to cut out your passport from the cut-out section at the back of this book.

2 Fold the passport in the middle, as shown above.

3 Fill in the information on the first page to make this passport personal to you!

4 At each stage in this book, you'll add **stickers** to your passport, showing the places you have visited.

PREPARE

Let's get ready for Hajj by learning about its history and virtues!

My Hajj PASSPORT

Name

Age

Country

Signature

Get a **Hajj & Umrah Visa** stamp on your passport from the stickers section. See Activity Number 2.

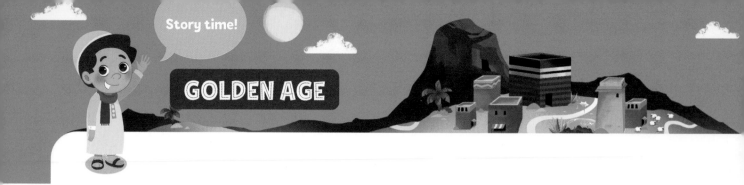

The History of Hajj

The sun blazed from a cloudless sky as millions of sparkles, like diamonds, glittered on the Zamzam water. Beside the well, Ismail 🕊 leaned against a rock as the faint rhythm of footsteps caught his attention. He put the arrows he had been sharpening aside as a familiar face beamed before him.

"Father!" he cried as he sprung to his feet. His face lit up with a huge smile. It was Ibrahim 🕊, the great Messenger of Allah. The two exchanged greetings. But Ismail 🕊 sensed there was more to this meeting.

"Allah has given me an order to build a house here," Ibrahim 🕊 said, pointing to a small hill nearby.

"Do what Allah has told you to do," said Ismail 🕊 without a moment's hesitation.

"Will you help me?" his father asked.

"I will indeed."

Ibrahim 🕊 smiled, and narrowing his eyes against the midday sun, he turned his face towards the small hill.

Stones were clustered around it as if someone had tried to build something there a long time ago. Otherwise, it was bare.

The pair walked towards the site, shading their eyes with their hands. After inspecting the spot for a moment, father and son started work.

Ismail 🕊 gathered the best stones he could find, while Ibrahim 🕊 placed them with expert care and without the need for cement to strengthen the building.

But as the walls got higher, they became impossible to reach. It was then that something amazing happened.

The Angel Jibreel 🕊 came down from the heavens with a stone from Jannah for Ibrahim 🕊 to stand on. Allah often sent Jibreel 🕊 when Ibrahim 🕊 needed help most.

→

The special stone rose like an elevator, allowing Ibrahim 🕊 to reach the tops of the walls.

As Ibrahim 🕊 used it to complete the building, the stone softened and a deep imprint of Ibrahim's 🕊 feet was engraved permanently into it. This stone is what we now know as 'Maqam Ibrahim' and is an important part of the Hajj rites.

For the final touch, Allah ordered Ibrahim 🕊 and Ismail 🕊 to leave a free space in one of the corners of the Kabah. The Angel Jibreel 🕊 came down again from the heavens with a different stone from Jannah to be placed as the cornerstone of the House of Allah. This is what we now know as 'Al-Hajr Al-Aswad' (The Black Stone).

Driven by faith and obedience, Ibrahim 🕊 and Ismail 🕊 completed the building of the Kabah.

"Our Lord," they said, as pearls of sweat ran down their faces, "Accept this service from us. You are the All Hearing, the All Knowing."

Allah ordered Ibrahim 🕊 to call people for Hajj. Although there was no one around the Kabah when Ibrahim 🕊 made the call, Allah assured him that people will come on foot and on every lean camel, and they will come from every deep and distant mountain highway.

Hajj is one of the five pillars of Islam. Today, millions of Muslims perform Hajj every year, answering the call of Ibrahim 🕊 and following the footsteps of the Prophet Muhammad 🕊, who showed us how to perform this great act of worship.

Much of the actions in Hajj follow the footsteps of the Prophet Ibrahim 🕊 and his family.

Principled Pillars

● Label the images below showing the five pillars of Islam. Use the *hadeeth* to help you. Which pillar will you be learning about in this book?

The Kabah is also known as the 'House of Allah' because He is remembered a lot there.

The Prophet ﷺ said:

"Islam has been built on five (pillars): testifying that there is no one worthy of worship except Allah and that Muhammad is the Messenger of Allah (shahadah), establishing the prayer, paying the Zakah, making Hajj to the House, and fasting Ramadan. (Bukhari & Muslim)

OBSERVATION SKILLS

PEACE OF HEART

Valuable Virtues

● Hajj has many great virtues. Use the *hadeeth* to help you fill in the two missing virtues before matching them all to their images using **stickers**.

Your dua is
accepted in Hajj.

Hajj gets rid of
poverty.

....
....

Hajj is one of the
best deeds in Islam.

You are the guest
of Allah when
on Hajj.

....
....

Hadeeth

The Prophet ﷺ said:

❝

The reward of Hajj (which is accepted by Allah) is nothing except Paradise. (Bukhari)

Whoever performs Hajj and doesn't do any evil there will return (free of sin) as the day his mother gave birth to him. (Bukhari)

PROBLEM SOLVING

SACRED RITES

When is Hajj?

● Use Aisha's clue to highlight the dates on the calendar when Hajj can be performed. With the help of a (grown-up), find out today's Islamic date and use it to find out how many days there are left for Hajj.

Muharram

```
            01  02  03  04
05  06  07  08  09  10  11
12  13  14  15  16  17  18
19  20  21  22  23  24  25
26  27  28  29
```

Safar

```
                01  02  03
04  05  06  07  08  09  10
11  12  13  14  15  16  17
18  19  20  21  22  23  24
25  26  27  28  29  30
```

Rabi I

```
                            01
02  03  04  05  06  07  08
09  10  11  12  13  14  15
16  17  18  19  20  21  22
23  24  25  26  27  28  29
```

Rabi II

```
01  02  03  04  05  06  07
08  09  10  11  12  13  14
15  16  17  18  19  20  21
22  23  24  25  26  27  28
29  30
```

Jumada I

```
        01  02  03  04  05
06  07  08  09  10  11  12
13  14  15  16  17  18  19
20  21  22  23  24  25  26
27  28  29
```

Jumada II

```
            01  02  03  04
05  06  07  08  09  10  11
12  13  14  15  16  17  18
19  20  21  22  23  24  25
26  27  28  29  30
```

> Hajj takes place for six days after the first week of the last month of the Islamic year.
>
> How many days are left for Hajj to begin?
>
> ....

Rajab

```
                01  02
03  04  05  06  07  08  09
10  11  12  13  14  15  16
17  18  19  20  21  22  23
24  25  26  27  28  29
```

Shaban

```
                        01
02  03  04  05  06  07  08
09  10  11  12  13  14  15
16  17  18  19  20  21  22
23  24  25  26  27  28  29
30
```

Ramadan

```
    01  02  03  04  05  06
07  08  09  10  11  12  13
14  15  16  17  18  19  20
21  22  23  24  25  26  27
28  29  30
```

Shawwal

```
            01  02  03  04
05  06  07  08  09  10  11
12  13  14  15  6   17  18
19  20  21  22  23  24  25
26  27  28  29
```

Dhul-Qa'dah

```
            01  02  03  04
05  06  07  08  09  10  11
12  13  14  15  16  17  18
19  20  21  22  23  24  25
26  27  28  29  30
```

Dhul-Hijjah

```
                            01
02  03  04  05  06  07  08
09  10  11  12  13  14  15
16  17  18  19  20  21  22
23  24  25  26  27  28  29
```

THINKING SKILLS

10 Glorious Days

● The first 10 days of Dhul-Hijjah are the best days of the year. Match the labels to the images and discover some of the good deeds Aisha can do in these blessed days.

Reciting Quran ◯

Reciting Takbeer, Tahleel and Tahmeed ◯

Salah ◯

Fasting ◯

Sadaqah ◯

Being Good to Parents ◯

Helping Others ◯

Performing Hajj ◯

The Prophet ﷺ said:

❝

No good deeds are better than what is done in these first ten days of Dhul-Hijjah. (Bukhari)

Hadeeth

SPIRITUAL INTELLIGENCE

PEACE OF HEART

Much Remembrance

● Read the *hadeeth* below about some of the best words of remembrance to say in the first ten days of Dhul-Hijjah. Then, match the words to their meanings and names.

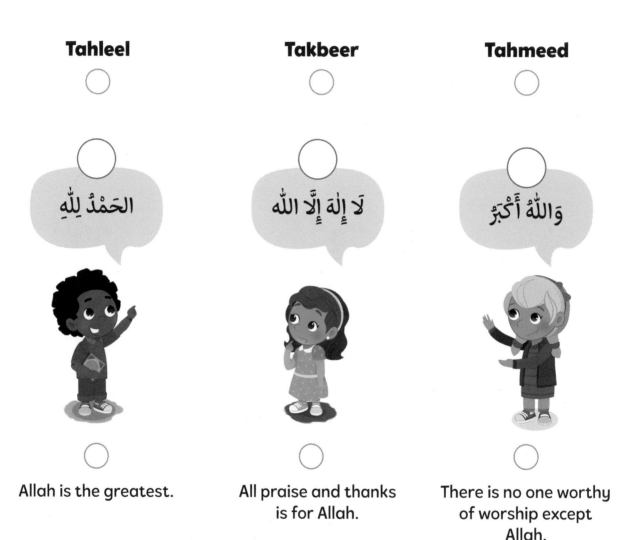

Tahleel	Takbeer	Tahmeed
○	○	○

اَلْحَمْدُ لِلّهِ

لَا إِلّهَ إِلَّا الله

وَاللّهُ أَكْبَرُ

Allah is the greatest.

All praise and thanks is for Allah.

There is no one worthy of worship except Allah.

The Prophet ﷺ said:

❝ *There are no days that are greater before Allah or in which good deeds are more beloved to Him than these ten days, so recite a great deal of tahleel, takbeer and tahmeed during them. (Ahmed)*

Hadeeth

SPIRITUAL INTELLIGENCE

SACRED RITES

Excuse Me Please

- Hajj should be performed at least once by Muslims if they are able to make it. Tick the characters that are excused from performing Hajj.

My brother is just a baby, so he doesn't have to go on Hajj.

I've been on Hajj already.

I have a serious long-term illness.

I'm really poor and can't afford to go on Hajj.

I'm have a mild temperature.

I'm going on holiday during the Hajj season.

THINKING SKILLS

SACRED RITES

Duty Calls

- There are many verses in the Quran about Hajj. Trace the dots to discover one of them below. Then with the help of a **grown-up**, find out which Surah this verse is found in. Can you find other verses discussing Hajj in the Quran?

وَلِلَّهِ عَلَى النَّاسِ حِجُّ الْبَيْتِ مَنِ اسْتَطَاعَ إِلَيْهِ سَبِيلًا

And it is the duty of mankind towards Allah to make pilgrimage to the House — for those who are able to make the journey

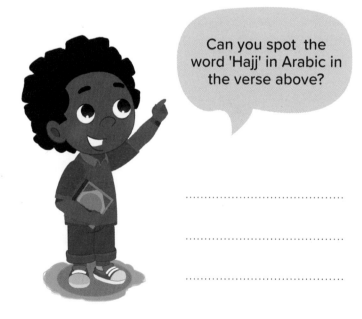

Can you spot the word 'Hajj' in Arabic in the verse above?

....

....

....

PEACE OF HEART

Honest Earning

• Only pure money can be used to go on Hajj. Tick the images that show ways in which money is earned in an honest and pure way.

Stolen Money

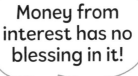

Money from interest has no blessing in it!

Interest Money

Money from Pure and Honest Work

Gambling

Selling Haram Items

Money from Cheating

Gifted Money

Halal Business

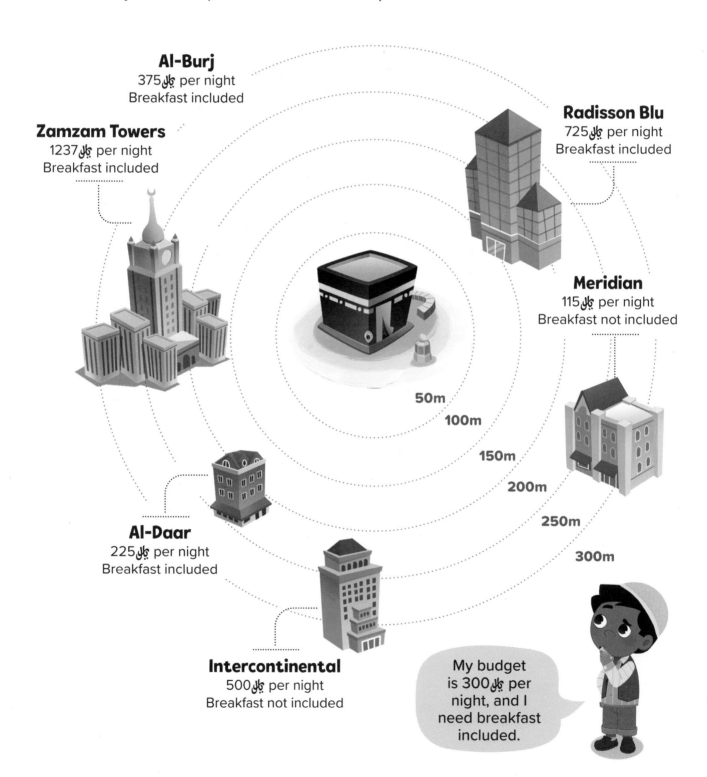

TRAVEL JOY

Enjoy Your Stay!

- Help Layth select a hotel that best meets his needs and is as close as possible to Masjid Al-Haram (where the Kabah is located).

Al-Burj
375﷼ per night
Breakfast included

Radisson Blu
725﷼ per night
Breakfast included

Zamzam Towers
1237﷼ per night
Breakfast included

Meridian
115﷼ per night
Breakfast not included

50m
100m
150m
200m
250m
300m

Al-Daar
225﷼ per night
Breakfast included

Intercontinental
500﷼ per night
Breakfast not included

My budget is 300﷼ per night, and I need breakfast included.

THINKING SKILLS

UMRAH

Let's get ready for Umrah. Think of it like a 'Mini-Hajj'.

Get the **Miqat** and **Makkah** stamps on your passport from the stickers section. See Activity Number 2.

SACRED RITES

Hajj Choices

● There are three different types of Hajj. Read the description of each type and match it to its image.

Tamattu'
Perform Umrah followed by Hajj whilst coming out of Ihram in between. This is best if you did not bring your sacrifice with you.

Ifrad
Performing Hajj only, without Umrah.

Qiraan
Perform Umrah followed by Hajj without coming out of Ihram in between.

THINKING SKILLS

SACRED RITES

Umrah Order

● Read the descriptions to order the images of the actions of Umrah correctly.

First, enter Ihram at the miqat.

After Tawaf, pray behind Maqam Ibrahim and drink Zamzam water

Upon entering Makkah, perform Tawaf.

Finally, shave your hair and exit Ihram.

After praying, perform Sa'ee.

Did you know that Umrah is known as the 'Little Hajj'?

OBSERVATION SKILLS

Ihram Limits

● During Hajj, a Muslim enters a special state called Ihram, in which there are certain things you cannot do. Discover what these actions are by circling the quadrilaterals (four-sided shapes below). Then, number those images using the descriptions.

1. Cutting Hair
2. Clipping Nails
3. Cover the Head
4. Hunting
5. Wearing Gloves
6. Applying Perfume

Simple Dress

● Qays will perform Hajj in simple, white, two-piece clothing called the Ihram dress. Use the **stickers** to dress Qays appropriately for when he enters the state of Ihram. Not all the stickers will be needed!

PEACE OF HEART

Answering the Call

- After entering Ihram, Zayd continually recites some special words called the 'Talbiyah'. Using the **stickers**, match the Arabic words to their correct translation to learn the meaning of the Talbiyah.

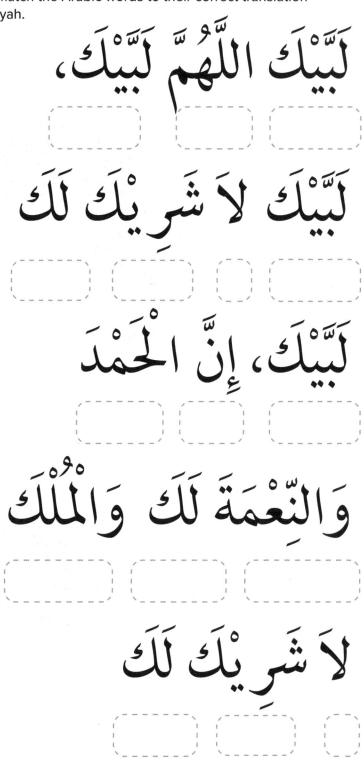

لَّبَّيْكَ اللَّهُمَّ لَبَّيْكَ،

لَّبَّيْكَ لاَ شَرِيْكَ لَكَ

لَّبَّيْكَ، إِنَّ الْحَمْدَ

وَالنَّعْمَةَ لَكَ وَالْمُلْكَ

لاَ شَرِيْكَ لَكَ

Meaning

Here I am, O Allah, here I am. Here I am; You have no partner, here I am. Indeed all praise and blessings are Yours, and all control. You have no partner.

Kabah Components

● Learn about the Kabah by numbering the descriptions to the correct areas.

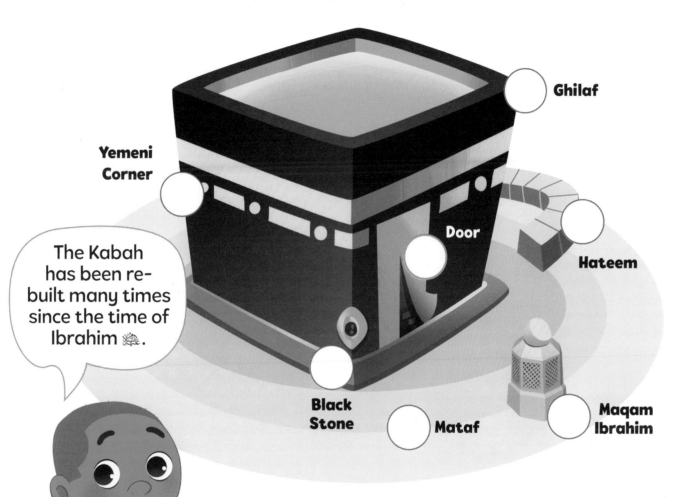

Ghilaf

Yemeni Corner

Door

Hateem

The Kabah has been re-built many times since the time of Ibrahim ﷺ.

Black Stone

Mataf

Maqam Ibrahim

1 It's recommended to touch this area on each round of Tawaf.

2 This is a stone from Jannah.

3 The Prophet Ibrahim used this to help build the Kabah.

4 The key to this has been held by the same tribe since the time of the Prophet ﷺ.

5 This is changed with a new piece every year.

6 This is the area where Tawaf is performed.

7 This area used to be part of the original Kabah.

Blessed Water

● Zamzam water is really special and has a lot of benefits. Use the hadeeth to discover its virtues and label the appropriate image.

....

....

....

....

The Prophet ﷺ said:

Hadeeth

" It (Zamzam) is a blessing, and it is food that nourishes. (Muslim)

The water of Zamzam is for whatever purpose it is drunk for. (Ibn Majah)

The Prophet ﷺ used ... to pour it over the sick and give it to them to drink. (At-Tirmidhi)

SPIRITUAL INTELLIGENCE

The Black Stone

● Learn about the amazing Black Stone by filling in the blanks.

The .... Stone is a stone from Jannah that was delivered by the Angel Jibreel at the time when Ibrahim .... was building the .... Allah ordered Ibrahim ﷺ to place the stone in the same position as it rests today on the corner of the Kabah. .... said, "The Black Stone came down from Jannah and was whiter than.............., then it became black by the sins of the children of Adam." At the time of the Prophet ﷺ, the stone was about .... , but today, only a few small..........................remain. The Black Stone marks the beginning and the end point of the Tawaf.

List of words

Black · Kabah · Muhammad ﷺ · milk

50cm long · pebbles · ﷺ

THINKING SKILLS

The Story of Sa'ee and Zamzam

"But why must you go?" Hajar said. After travelling for miles, she finally had the time to rest beside a rock. It was one of many in that valley, far from the places she was familiar with.

Ibrahim ﷺ remained quiet. She repeated the question a few more times, but her husband still gave no response.

"Oh, Ibrahim," she said, as she began to nurse her crying child. "Has Allah ordered you to leave us here?"

"Yes," her husband finally replied.

"Then He will not neglect us," said Hajar, as her face brightened with faith.

Without another word, Hajar watched her husband fade into the sea of sand. Ibrahim ﷺ turned his heart to Allah.

"Our Lord, I have settled my child in a valley of no vegetation, close to Your sanctified House, so that they may establish the prayer. So, make the hearts of people warm towards them, and provide them with fruits so that they may be grateful."

When Ibrahim ﷺ was no longer in sight, Hajar opened the leather bag he had left

→

for them. Inside were a bunch of dates and a small waterskin. She wondered how long these provisions would last. For days, there was not a sound but the whispers of the wind. But the day came when this silence was shattered by the cries of baby Ismail 🕊.

Hajar cradled her child as worry struck her when they finished their last drops of water. Not only was the valley barren, but now the waterskin was too. The hunger on Ismail's 🕊 face was as plain as day. Pained to see such agony, Hajar put Ismail 🕊 down and looked towards the bright sky and made dua to Allah for help.

Hajar looked around her and thought of a plan. She surveyed the land around her and spotted a small mountain nearby. She kissed Ismail's 🕊 forehead and left to seek help.

Her dress fluttered wildly in the wind. When she climbed the mountain, a smile brightened her weary face. She wiped the sweat off her temples, but her smile soon vanished. Nothing could be seen on the horizon except another mountain similar to the one she was on.

Hoping for help ahead, Hajar descended and made her way there. She clung dearly to her trust in Allah, even though all seemed lost.

When she reached the other mountain, there was still not a single person in sight. Sweat drenched her dress and her feet ached. This was not what she had hoped. Swallowing the air as if it were water, she tried to catch her breath.

With her baby crying in the distance, Hajar continued her effort. She sprang to her feet once again until a sound stopped her in her tracks. She was too tired to realise it was the seventh time she had covered the distance between the two mountains.

When she heard the sound again, she knew something was odd.

"Whoever you may be," she said, "have you got something to help me?"

She peered towards Ismail 🕊 and could not believe her eyes. An angel appeared, gleaming against the scorching sun. He raised his foot and struck the ground with his heel. Water gushed from the earth, like an oasis in the middle of the desert.

"Oh, Allah," she cried, rushing to the spring. "Praise be to You!"

She dug a basin in the ground, fearing that the water would stop. But it never did. Ismail 🕊 had his fill as the birds began to fly around the valley, breaking the hollow whispers of the wind.

Sa'ee Sprints

● Go between Mount Safa and Marwa while reciting the dua for Sa'ee at the end of each round. Can you memorise the whole dua by the time you've completed Sa'ee?

1 لَا إِلَهَ إِلَّا اللهُ وَحْدَهُ لَا شَرِيكَ لَهُ

2 لَهُ الْمُلْكُ وَلَهُ الْحَمْدُ

3 وَهُوَ عَلَى كُلِّ شَيْءٍ قَدِيرٌ

4 لَا إِلَهَ إِلَّا اللهُ وَحْدَهُ

5 أَنْجَزَ وَعْدَهُ

6 وَنَصَرَ عَبْدَهُ

7 وَهَزَمَ الْأَحْزَابَ وَحْدَهُ

HAJJ

It's time for the great days! You'll remember your Hajj for life!

Muzdalifah

Jamarat

Arafah

Mina

Get the **Arafah, Mina, Muzdalifah** and **Jamarat** stamps on your passport from the stickers section. See Activity Number 2.

Days of Hajj

● Label the date of each event in Hajj using the **stickers**. To help you, look for the date-tags next to the title of the activities in the pages that follow.

1

I'll enter Ihram once again for Hajj

2

I'll spend the night in Mina

3

I'll spend the day making dua in Arafah

5

I'll stone the big Jamarat

4

I'll spend the night in Muzdalifah

10

After Hajj, I'll perform Tawaf Al-Wida' before leaving Makkah

9

8

I'll stay in Mina and stone all three Jamarat

I'll perform Tawaf and Sa'ee

6

7

I'll shave my hair and come out of Ihram

I'll offer my sacrifice

Amazing Arafah

● Read the hadeeth about Arafah. Write the most amazing things you have learned about this special day.

The Prophet ﷺ said:

66

Indeed, Allah Almighty boasts to His angels of the pilgrims on the afternoon of the day of Arafah, saying: Look at My servants, coming to Me disheveled and dusty. (Ahmad) ● *The Hajj is Arafah. Whoever reaches the night of Arafah before the rising of the sun at dawn the next day, he has completed his pilgrimage. (Nasa'i)* ● *The best supplication is that which is made on the day of Arafah. The best of it is what was said by myself and the Prophets before me:*

لَا إِلَهَ إِلَّا اللَّهُ وَحْدَهُ لَا شَرِيكَ لَهُ، لَهُ الْمُلْكُ وَلَهُ الْحَمْدُ وَهُوَ عَلَى كُلِّ شَيْءٍ قَدِيرٌ

There is no one worthy of worship except Allah alone, without any partners, to Him belongs the dominion and all praise and He has power over all things. (At-Tirmidhi) ● *There is no day upon which Allah frees more of His servants from the Hellfire than the day of Arafah. He draws near and then He boasts of them to the angels, saying: "What do these servants want?" (Muslim)*

Hadeeth

That's a great dua to learn!

....

....

....

....

Orderly Eid

- Order the acts of worship that Thabit must perform on 10th Dhul-Hijjah. Use the descriptions to help you.

Next, you perform
your sacrifice.

First you stone
the big Jamarat.

Finally you perform
Tawaf and Sa'ee.

Before Tawaf, you
shave your hair.

THINKING SKILLS

A Difficult Decision

A dry leaf crunched under Ibrahim's 🕊 foot. Deep in thought, he turned to the boy walking beside him.

"My dear son," he said solemnly, "I have seen in a dream that I offered you as a sacrifice." The dream flashed in his mind as clear as day. It wasn't just a vision — it was an order from Allah.

"My dear father," said Ismail 🕊 without a moment's hesitation, "Do what you have been told. I'll be patient, in-sha-Allah."

Ibrahim's 🕊 heart was heavy at the thought of losing his son, who was just coming of age.

Ibrahim 🕊 stopped where he recognised the trees and shrubs. A small clearing lay before them as if it had waited for this very moment.

He gathered stones and piled them up. At one point, he paused with the thought of causing Ismail 🕊 pain. But it was the will of Allah. Ibrahim 🕊 carried on, placing the stones neatly above each other to make a platform.

With the stones in his hands, Ibrahim 🕊 remembered the incidents at Al-Aqaba in Makkah earlier that day. Passing by the area of Mina, a voice from a dark alley had caught him by surprise.

"Ibrahim," it whispered. "you don't have to do it. He is nothing but a child."

Ibrahim ﷺ had looked at the boy beside him with the love of a father. He would have taken a step back home, but another voice had stopped him.

"It's the devil, Ibrahim," it had said. Turning to where the voice had come from, Ibrahim saw an angel in gleaming light. "Stone him."

With the angel's advice, Ibrahim ﷺ had looked at the dry ground. Seeing that there were stones by his feet, he had bent down and picked them up one by one. Seven stones had darted towards the dark alley, and as if it were smoke, the figure vanished into thin air.

But just when they had thought that there was nothing but a clear path ahead of them, a voice from the next alley had caught them once again by surprise.

"Ibrahim," it whispered, "you don't have to do it. Your wife, Hajar, loves him so much."

This second instance was not the last time the devil had spoken to Ibrahim ﷺ.

"Ibrahim," it had said in the next alley, "you don't have to do it."

Even so, Ibrahim ﷺ had picked up stones by his feet on all three occasions, hurling seven stones at the dark figure. And just like smoke, it would vanish into thin air.

The thought of these incidents earlier in the day did nothing to shake Ibrahim's ﷺ faith. He placed the last of the stones on the platform. It was ready. Ismail ﷺ laid down. Ibrahim ﷺ looked at him intently. He took a deep breath and prepared to do what he would never have imagined.

"O Ibrahim!" a familiar voice pierced the tension, just as he was about to sacrifice his dear son. Ibrahim ﷺ turned towards the direction of the sound.

"You have fulfilled the dream," said the voice.

Ibrahim ﷺ wrapped his son safely in his arms as the pair witnessed a great, healthy ram appear. Ibrahim ﷺ sacrificed the animal, which served as a glorious feast to celebrate this great victory of faith.

(This story is mentioned in Tafseer At-Tabari on the authority of Ibn Abbas).

On Target

10th Dhul-Hijjah

● Drop your pencil and hit the Jamarat pillars. To make it harder, drop your pencil from a greater height.

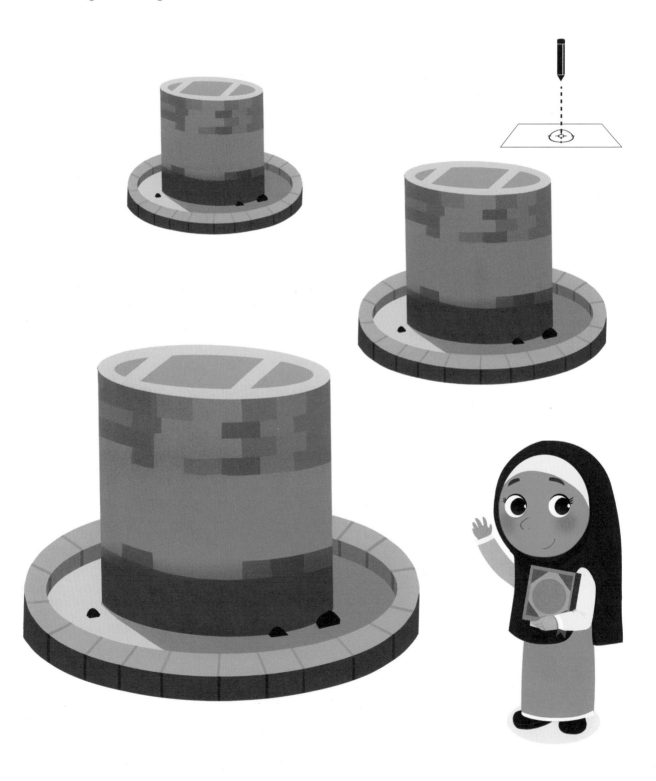

SACRED RITES

Mina Return

10th Dhul-Hijjah

The tenth day of Dhul-Hijjah is a busy time for Zayd. After performing Tawaf Al-Ifadah, he must return to Mina before midnight. Help him return as fast as possible without taking your pencil off the path. Note your times in the box below.

Time

Shared Sacrifice

● Even for those not going on Hajj, a Muslim household should perform a sacrifice during Eid Al-Adha. Match each character to a sacrifice that meets their budget.

My budget is 50 ﷼

238 ﷼

I can afford 70 ﷼

A camel and a cow can be shared by seven households.

329 ﷼

I have 35 ﷼

80 ﷼

I've got 80 ﷼

65 ﷼

PROBLEM SOLVING

Hajj Takbeer

● During the days of Hajj, the Takbeer is said after each prayer. Order the words of the Takbeer correctly by numbering the circles.

Days of Tanning

11-13th Dhul-Hijjah

After 10th Dhul-Hijjah, the families remain in Mina and stone the Jamarat pillars for three more days. Can you find the characters shown below?

OBSERVATION SKILLS

Make Your Hajj Scene

- Follow the steps below to set up your own 3D Hajj map. Then use the map to play out the rites of Hajj.

1 Find the fold-out Hajj scene at the back of this book and very carefully, tear it off on the perforated line.

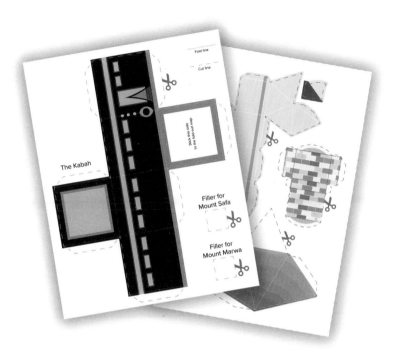

2 Find the cut-outs for the Hajj scene activity in the **Cut-out Section** at the back of this book.

3 Find the stickers for the Hajj scene activity in the **Stickers Section** at the back of this book.

www.learningroots.com/crafts

 See Hajj Scene Instructions

4 With the help of a grown-up, go online to the following website **www.LearningRoots.com/crafts** to see the instructions on how to make your exciting Hajj scene.

Lost in Tent City

The boys are taking different routes to reach their tent. Who is not likely to get there?

MADINAH

Visit the city of
the Prophet ﷺ.

Get the **Madinah** stamp
on your passport from
the stickers section.
See Activity Number 2.

SACRED RITES

The Prophet's City

Using the key to help you, match each symbol to an Arabic letter to reveal a famous site in Madinah. What does it say?

Connect the letters after finding them.

....

....

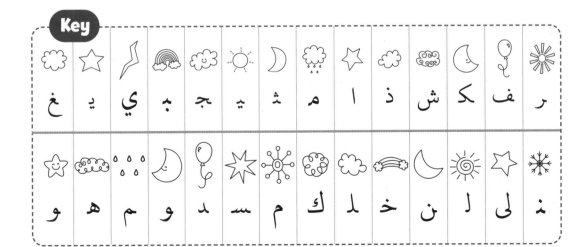

Key

☁	☆	⚡	🌈	☁	☀	🌙	🌧	⭐	☁	☁☁	🌙	🎈	✳
غ	يـ	ي	بـ	جـ	يـ	ثـ	مـ	ا	ذ	ش	كـ	ف	ر

⭐	☁	⠐	🌙	🎈	✦	❋	☁	☁	🌈	🌙	☀	☆	❄
و	هـ	مـ	د	سـ	مـ	كـ	لـ	خـ	نـ	لـ	ى	ذ	

LANGUAGE SKILLS

PEACE OF HEART

Garden of Paradise

● Using the **stickers**, complete this map of the different parts of Masjid An-Nabawi. Then, using the hadeeth to help you, mark the Rowda area with the green carpet sticker.

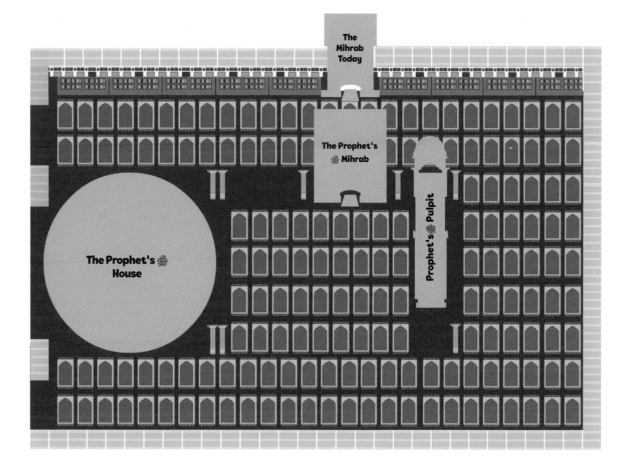

The Mihrab Today

The Prophet's Mihrab

Prophet's Pulpit

The Prophet's House

The Prophet ﷺ said:

"

Between my house and my pulpit lies a garden from the gardens of Paradise. (Bukhari)

Hadeeth

PEACE OF HEART

Saluting the Beloved

● Using the key to help you, put the correct vowels on the letters to complete the words said when the Prophet Muhammad's name is mentioned.

Now you can memorise these words too!

اللهم صل على محمد وعلى اله وصحبه وسلم

اللّٰهُمَّ صَلِّ
عَلَى مُحَمَّدٌ
وَعَلَى آلِه
وَصَحْبِهِ وَسَلِّمْ

Vowel Key

ّ	ه			و	َّ	ـ	ـٰ	ـ
َ		ِّ	َ					
⬒	⬣	◀	●	▲	◆	■	▼	★

GOLDEN AGE

Resting Place of the Greats

● Zayd visits the graveyard in Madinah called Baqi. Discover some of the Sahaba buried there by matching the Arabic names to the English using the **stickers** provided.

ٱلْعَبَّاس ٱبْنُ عَبْدِ ٱلْمُطَّلِبِ

The uncle of the Prophet Muhammad ﷺ

عَائِشَة بِنْت أَبِي بَكَر

The wife of the Prophet Muhammad ﷺ

عُثْمَان بن عَفَّان

The third Caliph

فَاطِمَة ٱبْنَت مُحَمَّد

The daughter of the Prophet Muhammad ﷺ

ٱلْحَسَن ٱبْن عَلِيّ ٱبْن أَبِي طَالِب

The grandson of the Prophet Muhammad ﷺ

FINE MOTOR SKILLS

GOLDEN AGE

Madinah's First Masjid

● Colour in this picture of Masjid Quba in Madinah.

The Prophet ﷺ said:

❝

Whoever purifies himself in his house, then comes to Masjid Quba and prays there, he will have the reward of 'Umrah. (Ibn Majah)

Hadeeth

CREATIVITY

Souvenir

● Aisha is shopping for gifts. Spot nine differences in this market in Madinah.

OBSERVATION SKILLS

Date Diversity

● Find the total cost of the dates Zayd wants to buy.

Ajwa	**Khudri**	**Safawi**	**Barhi**
6 ﷼ per kg	4.50 ﷼ per ½ kg	7 ﷼ per kg	3 ﷼ per ½ kg

 ....

I'm buying
2 kg of Ajwa
½ kg of Khudri
1½ kg of Safawi
1 kg of Bahri

 ....

....

 ....

....

SACRED RITES

Crossroads

● Complete the Hajj crossword using the clues below.

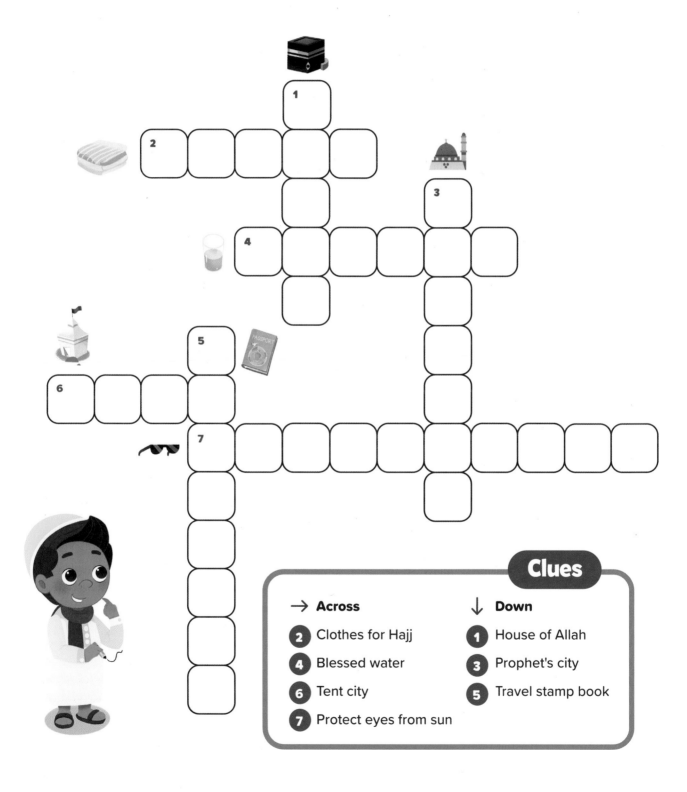

Clues

→ **Across**

2 Clothes for Hajj
4 Blessed water
6 Tent city
7 Protect eyes from sun

↓ **Down**

1 House of Allah
3 Prophet's city
5 Travel stamp book

GOLDEN AGE

Farewell Sermon

● Read the extract from the sermon that the Prophet ﷺ gave on Mount Arafah during his Farewell Hajj. Then, answer the questions.

1 What stood out most to you in this message?

....

2 What was the main message in this farewell speech?

....

3 What does this message reveal about the character of the Prophet ﷺ?

....

O People, lend me an attentive ear, for I don't know whether after this year I shall ever be among you again. So listen to what I am saying to you very carefully...

O People, just as you regard this month, this day, this city as sacred, so regard the life and property of every Muslim as a sacred trust.

Return the goods entrusted to you to their rightful owners. Hurt no one so that no one may hurt you. Remember that you will indeed meet your Lord, and that He will indeed reckon your deeds...

Beware of Shaytan, for the safety of your religion. He has lost hope in leading you astray in big things, so beware of following him in small things...

O People, listen to me carefully. Worship Allah, perform your five daily prayers, fast the month of Ramadan, and give your wealth in zakah. Perform Hajj if you can afford it.

All of mankind is from Adam and Hawwa, an Arab has no superiority over a non-Arab nor does a non-Arab have any superiority over an Arab; also a white person has no superiority over a black person nor does a black person have any superiority over a white person except by piety and good action.

Know that every Muslim is a brother to every Muslim and that the Muslims make up one brotherhood. A Muslim is not allowed to take something which belongs to a fellow Muslim unless it was given freely and willingly. Do not be unjust to yourselves.

Remember, one day you will appear before Allah and answer for your deeds. So beware, do not stray from the path of righteousness after I am gone...

I leave behind me two things, the Quran and my example, the Sunnah. If you follow these, you will never go astray.

Let all those who listen to me pass on my words to others...

Be my witness, O Allah, that I have conveyed Your message to Your people.

Neat work!

TRAVEL JOY

Hajj Search

Qays is reviewing the names of the places he visited while on Hajj. Help him find the list of words below.

```
E B B D E J Q K N Z T W H M Z P
Q M Y Q I B U E R R X V A N I M
G P J N Z Z B H I D A K F L T X
P M I B I E K U F N K P I A W T
E S A F A A N H X A Z R L C K E
Q V D D I Z W C H D H B A F G Q
P M G I I C B L F L F B D D Q V
K Y S Y O N X X T K S B Z Q Z V
Y H R M U U A L D V A D U M B D
X Q H R V Y J H A K I B M E O T
L K F J U Y O B N R S E A L X R
K W G Q U B A P C W A A W H G B
D L Q L X X X D O P R F R Z O N
Z K L M X J U I J E D D A H C X
Y A F F J H H T O Y D C M H S D
U A B F U D G T M A P F B Y M D
```

1. Mina
2. Arafah
3. Muzdalifah
4. Safa
5. Marwa
6. Kabah
7. Quba
8. Madinah
9. Jeddah
10. Makkah
11. Juhfah
12. Uhud

OBSERVATION SKILLS

ANSWERS

**To see the answers
to the activities in this book,
please visit:**

LearningRoots.com/answers

CUT-OUT SECTION

my Hajj
PASSPORT

Passport Name and Details

Name

Age

Country

Signature

Photo

Make Your Hajj Scene

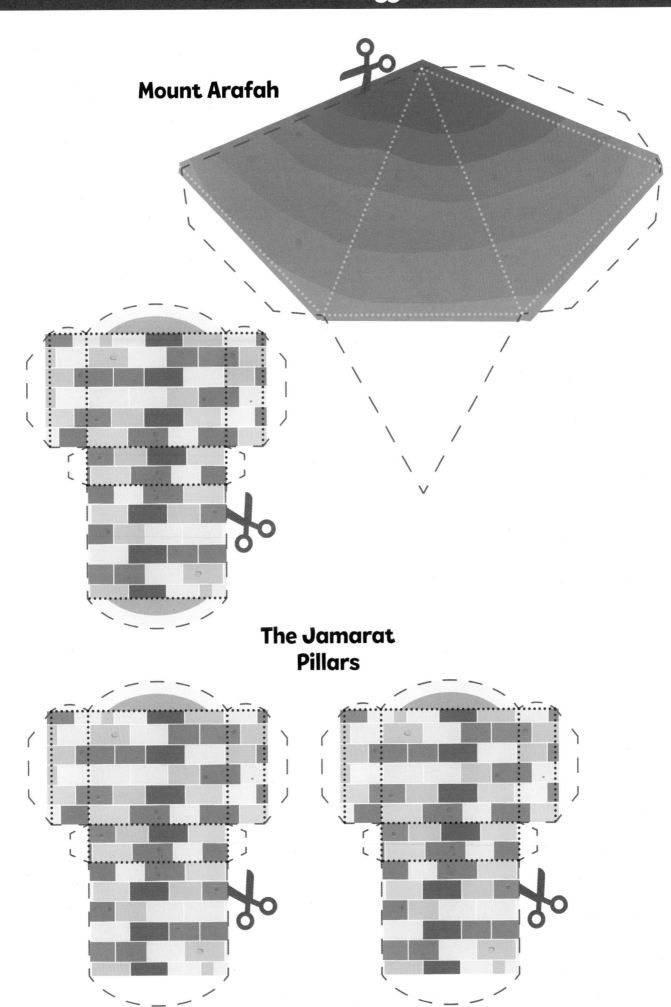

Mount Arafah

**The Jamarat
Pillars**

 Learning Roots
Cut-Out Activity

 Learning Roots
Cut-Out Activity

 Learning Roots
Cut-Out Activity

 Learning Roots
Cut-Out Activity

 Learning Roots
Cut-Out Activity

 Learning Roots
Cut-Out Activity

 Learning Roots
Cut-Out Activity

 Learning Roots
Cut-Out Activity

 Learning Roots
Cut-Out Activity

 Learning Roots
Cut-Out Activity

 Learning Roots
Cut-Out Activity

 Learning Roots
Cut-Out Activity

 Learning Roots
Cut-Out Activity

 Learning Roots
Cut-Out Activity

 Learning Roots
Cut-Out Activity

 Learning Roots
Cut-Out Activity

 Learning Roots
Cut-Out Activity

 Learning Roots
Cut-Out Activity

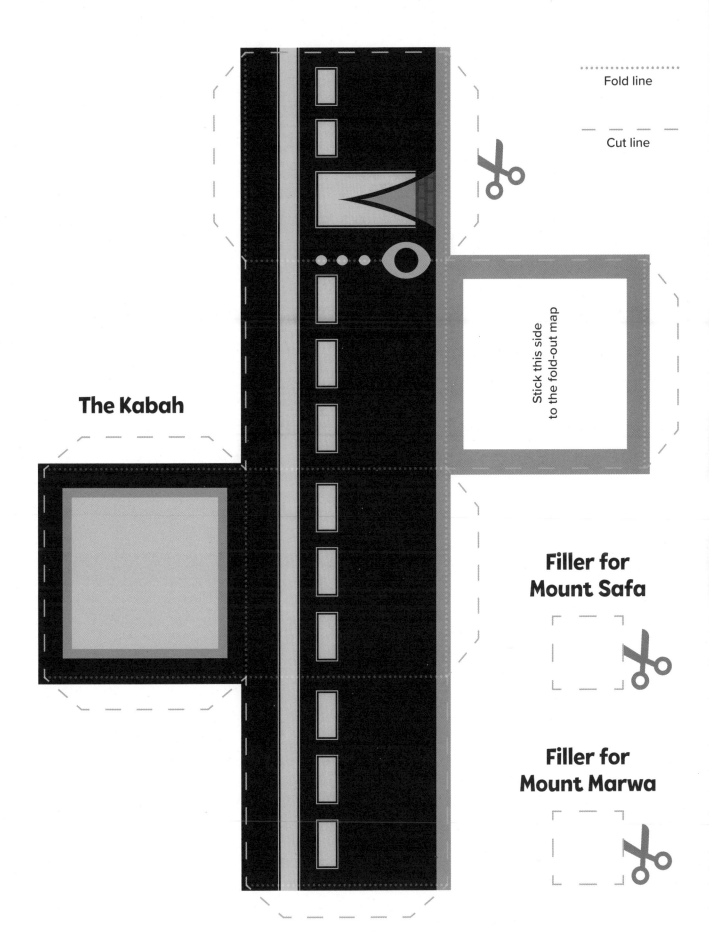

Fold line

Cut line

The Kabah

Stick this side
to the fold-out map

Filler for
Mount Safa

Filler for
Mount Marwa

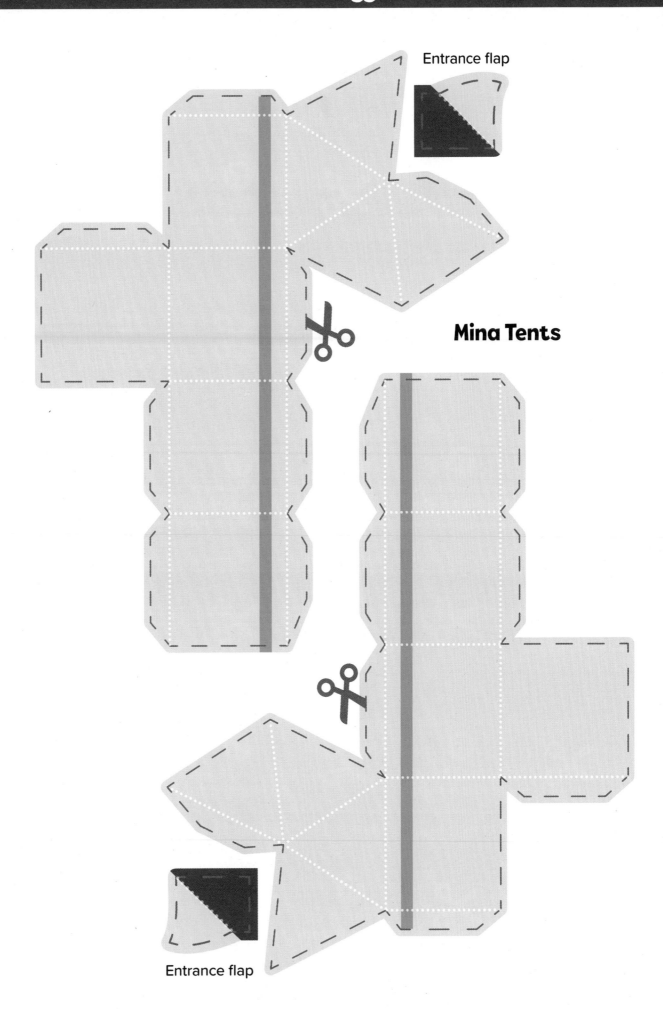

Entrance flap

Mina Tents

Entrance flap

 Learning Roots **Cut-Out Activity**

 Learning Roots **Cut-Out Activity**

 Learning Roots **Cut-Out Activity**

 Learning Roots **Cut-Out Activity**
Learning Roots **Cut-Out Activity**
Learning Roots **Cut-Out Activity**

 Learning Roots **Cut-Out Activity**

 Learning Roots **Cut-Out Activity**
Learning Roots **Cut-Out Activity**

Learning Roots **Cut-Out Activity**
 Learning Roots **Cut-Out Activity**
 Learning Roots **Cut-Out Activity**

 Learning Roots **Cut-Out Activity**
 Learning Roots **Cut-Out Activity**
 Learning Roots **Cut-Out Activity**

 Learning Roots **Cut-Out Activity**
 Learning Roots **Cut-Out Activity**
Learning Roots **Cut-Out Activity**

 Learning Roots **Cut-Out Activity**

 Learning Roots **Cut-Out Activity**
Learning Roots **Cut-Out Activity**

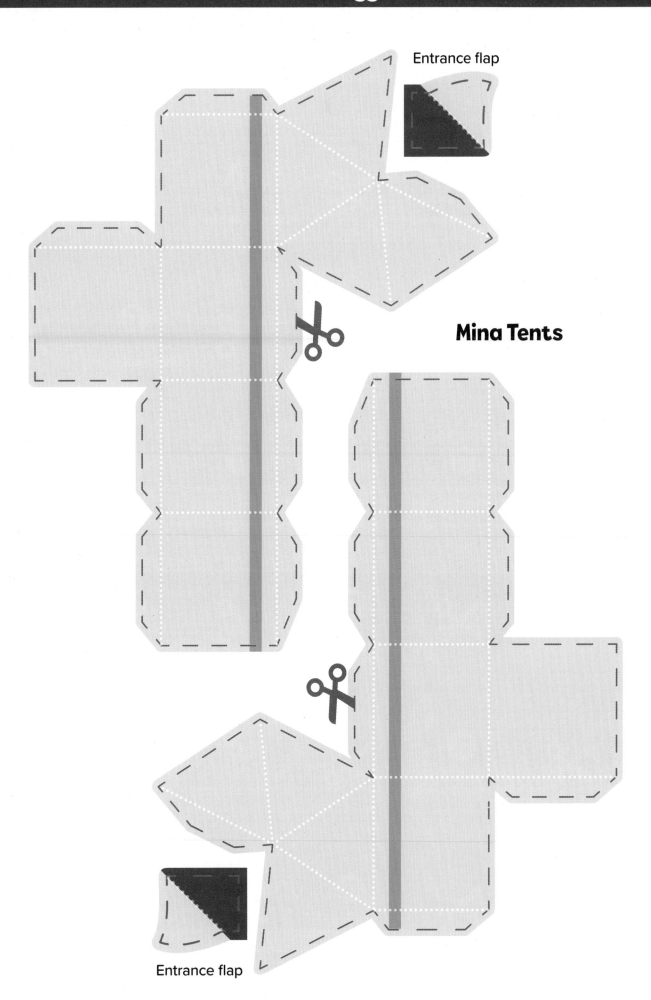

Entrance flap

Mina Tents

Entrance flap

STICKERS SECTION

FEEDBACK PLEASE!

We would love to hear your thoughts on this book. Please let us know at:

LearningRoots.com/Feedback